TODAY
I WILL LISTEN

Journal for Reflection, Inspiration, and Growth

MARVA SHAND-MCINTOSH

Founder of *I Love to Listen Day*

THIS JOURNAL BELONGS TO

Today I Will Listen

Today, I will listen
Without interrupting
Without prejudging
Without second-guessing
Without gazing
Without rehearsing
Without discounting
Without filtering
Without correcting
Without contradicting
Today I will just listen

Today I will listen
With attention
With humility
With respect
With patience
With understanding
With awe
With gladness
With empathy
With warmth
With gratitude
With reverence
Today, I will just listen

This poem was written in celebration of
I Love to Listen Day: **May 16th**.

ACKNOWLEDGEMENTS

Writing "Today I Will Listen: A Journal for Reflection, Inspiration, and Growth" has been a journey of self-discovery, creativity, and profound reflection. I could not have completed this project without the unwavering support, encouragement, and inspiration from a multitude of incredible individuals and sources.

First and foremost, I am deeply grateful to my son, Juwanza McIntosh and my other family members for their enduring love and support throughout this endeavor. Your patience, understanding, and belief in me provided the foundation upon which I built this book. Thank you for being my constant source of strength.

To my friends and peers, your encouragement and enthusiasm for this project have been invaluable. Your willingness to lend an ear, share your thoughts, and offer constructive feedback has been instrumental in shaping the pages of this journal.

A heartfelt thank you to my writing coach, Mary Lou Reid and my editor, Leisa Premdas whose guidance helped me navigate the challenging waters of the creative process. Your insights and wisdom were the compass that steered me towards my creative destination.

I extend my gratitude to the countless authors, thinkers, and philosophers whose works have enriched my understanding of the art of listening and personal growth. Your words have been a wellspring of inspiration and have deeply influenced the content of this journal.

I am indebted to the team at Book Baby for believing in the vision of "Today I Will Listen" and for their unwavering dedication to bringing this project to life. Your professionalism, expertise, and passion for literature have made this dream a reality.

Last and most importantly, to the readers who pick up this journal, may its pages serve as a source of reflection, inspiration, and personal growth in your own lives. Your willingness to embark on this listening journey is a testament to the power of curiosity and self-improvement.

In the spirit of listening, I extend my heartfelt appreciation to each and every one of you who contributed to the creation of "Today I Will Listen." May the act of listening continue to bring us closer to ourselves and to one another.

With gratitude,
Marva Shand-McIntosh

LISTENING QUOTES BY MARVA SHAND-MCINTOSH

Today, I Will Listen: A Journal of Reflection, Inspiration, and Growth belongs to you! It is chock full of originality by way of listening quotes, a poem, and an affirmation to help you clarify the meaning and measure of your listening endeavors. The journal is the perfect space to explore and express your own listening journey with the same unbridled freedom, creativity, and style that inspired these authentic works of art.

The poem in this journal was written to celebrate *I Love to Listen Day* recognized worldwide on **May 16th** and reflects my efforts to distill some of the ideals of listening into actionable points. This poem, "Today I Will Listen," has been read on seven continents and translated into several languages, thus making it the ideal prompt for your journal.

We are born listeners.

If you want to change the world,
go home and listen to your family.

Listening is a spiritual discipline.

Be patient with each other because
we all have listening challenges.

Listen by design and create
a listening culture where you are.

Let listening be your brand.

Caring looks and feels like listening.

Be your own Chief Listening Officer.

Listening is not intuitive.
It is a discipline that requires much restraint.

Listening is a team sport.

Listen: that's what smart people do.

Listen: that's what effective leaders do.

Listen: that's what loving partners do.

Your listening cannot be misquoted.

Dear leaders, listening is not just for children and subordinates.

He or she who listens first is the leader.

Listening is to humanity
what sunshine is to a flower.

Listening doesn't have to be
perfect to be powerful.

Not listening is not clever.

Listen with the intent to be kind.

Listening is a mark of intelligence from
the first century to the present.

Listening is the first communication
skill that we learn. It is the foundation
of all our communications.

Human beings have an insatiable desire
to feel understood.

Listening doesn't require expertise;
it requires humanity.

Listening to understand is loving kindness.

The gift of listening is a gift of love.

Today, be the first to listen and always listen first.

We all have the ability to listen;
the difference is how well we use it.

Listen and be the reason that someone
feels understood.

When we listen, we empower others.

Today, I will listen to the people in front of me.

Listening is strength under control.

Listening is service above self.

Show up as your authentic self and listen
the best way you know how.

Listening is not a spare tire that we pull out in times of conflict and trouble. It is the steering wheel that directs us on life's journey.

Kindness is listening to someone who cannot repay you for your time and attention.

I will always be relevant if I will only listen first.

There is no substitute, replacement, proxy, or surrogate for listening.

You may not always see the results
of your listening service, but every bit
of listening energy that you contribute
to the world makes it a better place for all.

Effective leaders lead and love by listening.

A listening life doesn't happen by chance.

Our closest relationships require
the greatest need for listening.

Listen carefully before offering advice.

Read and share stories about
exemplary listeners throughout history.

Whether I'm a good listener or not,
I'm a listening role model.

No matter what your communication
interaction is like, be quick to listen.

The most efficient way to train the tongue
is to train the ear to patiently listen.

How does my listening attitude define me?

Listening is not glamorous; it is essential.

Listening is a different way to be smart and kind.

Does listening run in your family?

Listening is the most transferable
communication skill. Once learned, we can apply
it to every aspect of our lives.

Listening saves lives, money,
opportunities, and relationships.

Create a listening culture in your space by providing **Exemplary Listening Awards**.

Listening is priceless.

Treasure the listener(s) in your life.

If you haven't listened, you shouldn't speak.

How have you prioritized the development
of your listening skills?

You are in charge of your listening story.
It is what becomes your listening legacy.

In most conversations, the louder the yelling, the greater the misunderstanding. Try listening.

Listeners are the kind of leaders whom
others love to willingly follow.

Don't just hear. Listen.

The strongest people are those who are still listening to others after they themselves have been feeling misunderstood and unheard.

A listener is the one who leaves a mark
but not a scar.

Teach the child to listen well, and it will not be necessary to penalize the man.

Empathetic listening is the most
underrated means of change in the world.

Speak up for listening.

Share the power of listening with everyone
because there is a listening tree
in every listening seed that is planted.

Don't lose your ability to listen to the people who are in front of you.

By listening, leaders provide a safe place
for youth to express and defend their emotions,
opinions, and deep insights.

There is no effective communication
without listening.

I will give the gift of listening while I can still hear.

147

A listening champion embraces the power of listening and shares that gift with others.

Guard your listening reputation by practicing
what you've learned about listening.

You may not always see the results
of your listening service, but every bit of listening
energy that you contribute to the world makes
it a better place for all of us.

Yes, listening matters.

Listening is one of the most
desired expressions of love.

Listening with intention
comes by design, not by default.

There's no applause for the gift of listening,
but when one feels understood, that heart gives
a quiet standing ovation of gratitude.

Listening is the road that leads to inclusion.

Listening is paying it forward.

A listening blind spot will lead to communication crashes.

The listening effect causes ordinary people to have extraordinary impact in the world.

Listening leads to a communication bridge.
Not listening leads to a communication wall.

Listening is given as a service
and accepted as a gift.

Listening is not a soft skill; it is a power skill.

Listen because everyone speaks two languages.
Each speaks body language and a native language.

Listening is always good for business.

Listening is like a muscle. The more you practice, the stronger it becomes.

Your listening is your trademark and your logo.

Listen as if your life depends
on it because it does.

There is no perfect listener,
so be kind to your listening self.

Listening is a global solution to a global problem.

Listen well but don't be silenced.

The ears do not hear what the mind
does not want to know.

Listening is how we demonstrate
love in action rather than just words.

People grow when they feel understood.
If you want to help someone heal,
listen to him without an agenda.

Listen is an intangible verb with tangible effects.

Listening is the critical cornerstone to our children's early language development.

Listen to yourself; cursing others
will never bring healing to you.

The Listening Affirmation

"May you always have
one true listener in your life
and
May you always strive to be
that one true listener in someone's life."

MARVA SHAND-MCINTOSH

Meet Marva Shand-McIntosh, a changemaker and visionary who has dedicated her life to the transformative power of listening. As the founder of I Love to Listen Day, the premier international listening event celebrated annually on May 16th, Shand-McIntosh has emerged as a leading advocate for the unheard.

Drawing from over three decades of experience as an accomplished speech-language pathologist in Washington, D.C., Shand-McIntosh weaves together insights and stories that reflect her deep understanding of the profound impact of listening on individuals and communities. Her work extends beyond the pages of her books, as she operates on multiple fronts as an author, lecturer, and certified listening professional.

Shand-McIntosh's commitment to her cause has not gone unnoticed, as she has been honored with several prestigious awards. In 2013, she received the Distinguished Leadership Award from the District of Columbia Speech-Language Hearing Association, and in 2014, she was recognized with the Distinguished Educator Award from the International Listening Association.

Beyond her written work and accolades, Shand-McIntosh actively contributes to the field, serving as a vice president for the International Listening Association and holding positions on the executive boards of three other educational institutions. Her influence extends nationally and internationally, leaving an indelible mark on the importance of listening as a catalyst for positive change.

In this indispensable listening journal, Marva Shand-McIntosh invites you to join her on a journey of discovery, highlighting the profound impact that intentional listening can have on our lives and the world around us.